T0128709

New
BEGINNING
STEP BY STEP GUIDE
TO NEWBIRTH

BRENDA DUCKWORTH

authorHOUSE®

AuthorHouse™
1663 Liberty Drive
Bloomington, IN 47403
www.authorhouse.com
Phone: 1 (800) 839-8640

Published by AuthorHouse   03/21/2017

ISBN: 978-1-5246-5664-5 (sc)
ISBN: 978-1-5246-5665-2 (hc)
ISBN: 978-1-5246-5666-9 (e)

Library of Congress Control Number: 2016921124

Print information available on the last page.

Any people depicted in stock imagery provided by Thinkstock are models,
and such images are being used for illustrative purposes only.
Certain stock imagery © Thinkstock.

This book is printed on acid-free paper.

Because of the dynamic nature of the Internet, any web addresses or links contained in
this book may have changed since publication and may no longer be valid. The views
expressed in this work are solely those of the author and do not necessarily reflect the
views of the publisher, and the publisher hereby disclaims any responsibility for them.

NKJV:

Scripture taken from the New King James Version®. Copyright © 1982
by Thomas Nelson. Used by permission. All rights reserved.

Step-By-Step Self-Help Guide to New Life in Christ

New Birth in Christ

To God, the One and only One, who has given me the inspired message in this book

Acknowledgements

My parents, especially my mother Corine Gage, who taught me about Jesus. My loving husband, he has always pushed and supported me in publishing this book. And last, but not least, I want to thank my children, Raquel, Dalfon, Ben, Alaine, and my grandchildren, Dion Jr., Monica, Jordan, Aaliyah, Amya, and Amari.

With all my heart, I give thanks to my church family at Disciples of Christ International Ministries of Bakersfield, who stayed with us through thick and thin and are presently with us.

Contents

About the Author

I, Brenda L. Duckworth, was born in Marvell, Arkansas and I am the daughter of share croppers. I gave my heart to the Lord at the age of twelve and received the Holy Spirit. I was the tenth child of thirteen children. I, along with my brother Derrick, attended the segregated elementary school the first year of segregation. I moved to California in 1969, at age fourteen, where I continued my education. God would use me in many ways but I was not aware of it as being a gift from God. As life became more and more challenging, I needed more and more answers; therefore I began to seek God for wisdom and revelation. I am the mother of three and the grandmother of six. My husband and I have devoted our lives to seeing the people in the community grow and mature in the things of God by giving pastoral care to many.

About the book

This book is a word-testimony of the steps to new birth in Christ. It is written in the terms of the beginning of natural life starting from conception and continuing into adulthood. Every stage is different, but continual, and so is the new birth in Christ. It is powerful and will lead you to your purpose and the direction in order to stay on course to your eternal destiny. Not only will you find your purpose, but the awareness of grace, forgiveness, power, benefits, God given gifts and talents are discovered as well. In my journey of pastoring for sixteen years, I found that many people were lacking the knowledge that is in this book.

Introduction

In life experiences many speak the phrases, "I am a good person", "I do not need to be born-again," or "it does not take all that." Well I'm here to say it does take all that God said it would take and all that Jesus died for. Usually, when one make those statements, it means that he or she is living by his or her own standards or righteousness. Jesus said that no one was good except God alone (Mark 10:18). The Bible clearly talks about being "born-again."

In the bible Jesus let us know that we must be born-again.
He spoke to a man named Nicodemus concerning being
born-again.

*John 3:1-7 "There was a man of the Pharisees named
Nicodemus, a ruler of the Jews. This man came to Jesus by
night and said to Him, "Rabbi, we know that you are a
teacher come from God; for no one can do these signs that
you do unless God is with him." Jesus answered and said
to him, "Most assuredly, I say to you, unless one is born
again, he cannot see the kingdom of God." Nicodemus said
to Him, "How can a man be born when he is old? Can he
enter a second time into his mother's womb and be born?"
Jesus answered, "Most assuredly, I say to you, unless one is
born of water and the Spirit, he cannot enter the kingdom
of God. That which is born of the flesh is flesh, and that
which is born of the Spirit is spirit. Do not marvel that I
said to you, "You must be born again."*

Without being born-again, we miss the mark that God
intended for us (Rom. 3:23). God set forth a purpose for
us before we were placed into our mother's womb. In the
book of Jeremiah, God told him that He knew him before

he was formed into his mother's womb. God foreknew him, just as He foreknew you.

> *Jeremiah 1:4-5 says, The word of the Lord came to me, saying, "Before I formed you in the womb I knew you, before you were born I set you apart; I appointed you as a prophet to the nations."*

God has plans for us, which are good and not evil. However, if we are not born-again, we will miss the perfect plans of God (Jer. 29:11). When we miss the plans of God, it usually results in calamity, destruction, or unfruitfulness.

For instance, I have missed the mark of God many times in my decisions that I made without Him and they all resulted in hurt and ruin. They were unfruitful in the flesh but a testimony in the spirit. This is one of the reasons why I am so thankful that God allowed me to write this book.

I was one of those "good people." I am a living testimony that you must be born-again. When I became born again,

I was twelve years old and my life changed from that day forward. My mother was saved and I always had a sense of God's righteousness.

After I was born-again, I wanted to please God more than I wanted to appease myself. Even when I was unaware of it, God was still with me helping me make quality decisions that has preserved me this far. I am still going to him for answers at the blessed age of sixty-one. God will re-direct your life.

I could go on and on with missing the mark of God in my life, including; making decisions concerning relationships, parenting, career, and day-to-day situations. But, with new birth, God will redirect us to the path He intended for us, if we acknowledge him (Prov. 3:6).

God Will Redirect Our Lives

I missed the mark by getting married to a non-believer and having children with that union. God redirected my life and blessed me with a husband of His choice, the one I have been married to for the past twenty-five years and all of my children are Christians as a result of being re-directed. However, the pain of missing the mark of God hurts and leaves scars.

Again, the statement or belief that one does not need to be born-again, is just simply not the truth according to the gospel of Jesus Christ (John 3:1-3). In the book of Jeremiah, God spoke to Jeremiah concerning His plans He had for him; God also has plans just for you. Jesus made the way so the plans God has for us will manifest through His birth, death, and resurrection. God re-directs us to Him and His plans He has for us, this is our infant stage.

Jeremiah 29:11 says, "For I know the thoughts that I think toward you, says the Lord, thoughts of peace and not of evil, to give you a future and a hope."

The purpose of being born-again is the means in which God re-direct us to him and his plans he has for us, this is our infant stage.

Being born again, having the indwelling of the Holy Spirit, gives us access to God and is our means of fellowshipping with Him. We communicate with Him in Spirit and in Truth. Our fellowship with God is through the spirit. If we have not been born of his Spirit, we will not enter into the kingdom of God. "Fellowship with God" is hearing God and doing what He has purposed us to do.

The phrase "I am a good person" usually comes from the person who says "I have my own relationship with God," But God is not asking for a relationship, He desires "fellowship" with His people. When you are in fellowship with God, He reveals your purpose to you, and you share in His Glory, which means you are blessed and He is glorified.

Relationship—is defined as the way in which two or more people or things are connected. It is also a state of affairs existing between those having relations or dealings. Fellowship—is defined as companionship, or company. It is a community of interest, activity, feeling, or experience. It is the state of being a fellow.

When you have fellowship with Him by the indwelling of the Holy Spirit, God's own Spirit, it gives you power to live a saved life and to be a witness for Him (Acts 1:8). Having a relationship with Him could be a connection of any kind, such as knowing of His creation, however, having fellowship with Him means you are sharing with Him, "a community interest". Therefore; being born-again causes you to share in His supernatural power, being "spirit-led".

Acts 1:8 says, "But you will receive power when the Holy Spirit comes on you; and you will be my witnesses in Jerusalem, and in all Judea and Samaria, and to the ends of the earth."

Without the Holy Spirit, we are powerless. It has been clearly stated (John 3:1-7) that we must be born again in order to receive the purposed things of God (His Kingdom). We all are blessed, God blessed us when He created us (Gen. 1:26-28). Being blessed and living out your God given purpose are two different things. Jesus even said, "no one is good but God"; if Jesus did not consider Himself "good" how is it that we consider ourselves good without the leading of the Holy Spirit (Rom. 7:13-21)?

Matthew 19:16-17 says, "Now behold, one came and said to Him, "Good Teacher, what good thing shall I do that I may have eternal life?" So He said to him, "Why do you call Me good? No one is good but One, that is, God. But if you want to enter into life, keep the commandments."

The significance of being born-again is necessary to enter into the kingdom of God (God's purpose for your life). This question enters our mind often, "Who gives new birth?" the answer is God. He gives His own Spirit, which manifests in new life. God so loved the world (people who were not following God) that He gave His only begotten son, and His son gave His life. And because His son gave His life, we were able to receive the Holy Spirit, a gift from God. The phrase "new birth" or being born-again is all about love and giving, God gave His son, and His son gave His life.

John 3:16-17 says "For God so loved the world that he gave his one and only Son, that whoever believes in him shall not perish but have eternal life. For God did not send his Son into the world to condemn the world, but to save the world through him."

God gave His son to fulfill a purpose, and Jesus gave His life to fulfill a promise for us. Because Jesus died, it gave us grace to receive the free gift of the Holy Spirit (John 14:16-8).

John 16:7 says, "Nevertheless I tell you the truth. It is to your advantage that I go away; for if I do not go away, the Helper will not come to you; but if I depart, I will send Him to you."

Jesus did the finishing work so we could receive God's Spirit, which gives us our "new birth." When we say "born-again of the spirit," we are saying we have just come into the purposed things of God and not of the flesh of the birth of our parents. Jesus gave up His life to ensure our new birth, our seal of promise for eternal life.

When Jesus cried out with a loud voice, it indicated that they did not kill Him, He finished His purpose on earth, to give His life. Usually the first thing that leaves when a man is dying is his voice, Jesus had a voice and He allowed everyone to know by crying out with it.

Mark 15:34-37 says "And at the ninth hour Jesus cried out with a loud voice, saying, "Eloi, Eloi, lama sabachthani?" which is translated, "My God, My God, why have you forsaken me?" And Jesus cried out with a loud voice, and breathed His last."

Chapter 1

Making a Quality Decision (The Conception Stage)

Before a child is born, things are happening before the actual birth, specifically five things must occur before the "spiritual birth". This is like the conception of a pregnant woman.

These things must go on before your spiritual birth, being born-again of God's Holy Spirit, according to scripture:

1. Hear the Word of God
   ## Concerning Jesus Christ

In the Old Testament, the prophets spoke of Jesus's coming, also In the New Testament. In the New Testament the prophecies were fulfilled concerning His birth, crucifixion, and resurrection. There are many prophecies throughout the Old Testament concerning the coming of Jesus Christ; B C. which stands for before Christ came.

Isaiah 9:6 says "For to us a child is born, to us a son is given, and the government will be on his shoulders. And he will be called Wonderful Counselor, Mighty God, Everlasting Father, Prince of Peace."

The gospels of Jesus Christ—Matthew, Mark, Luke, and John and specially (John 3:16-17, and 1 Peter 1:23-24) also provides evidence.

2. Believe the Word

Faith is to believe without any material evidence. The gospel of Jesus is, His birth from a virgin, ministry, crucifixion, burial, and resurrection (God raised Him from the dead). The gospels—Matthew, Mark, Luke, and John. The Gospel was preached in Acts 8:12-13; Romans 3:22, and in Romans 10:9-10 that also provides evidence.

3. Admit That You Have Sinned

In the book of Romans 3:23 and 1 John 1:8, talks about falling short of the Glory of God and confessing our sins to God. This is realizing that our ways and our thoughts are not like God's and we need a savior. God desires your personal admission of sins. Once we realize that we have sinned, God is faithful and just to forgive and cleanse us from all of the unrighteousness.

We all have sinned and fallen short of what God intended for us. Making the statements "I do not need to be born-again," "I am a good person," or "I do not need all of that" is simply not the truth. Repentance must take place before we receive the "free gift", the Holy Spirit. John the Baptist, Jesus, and the disciples all taught repentance.

4. Repent and Be Converted

This is changing your way of thinking, because of the remorse of past actions, to God's way of thinking. This is accomplished by studying and obeying the Word of God. Repent is to feel or show that you are sorry for something bad or wrong that you did and you want to do what is right. It is to turn from sin and dedicate oneself to the amendments of one's life. It is to feel regret or contrition.

5. Invite Jesus into Your Life

No one can force you, It must be on your own free will to accept Jesus as Lord, not just as "savior". Jesus is the savior of the world, whether you believe it or not, He has already died for the world (John-3:16-18). It is your decision to believe in Him as Lord of your life and invite Him in to direct your path. (Invite—is to request the presence or participation of or to urge politely).

After knowing you must be born-again, and hearing about Jesus Christ, our Lord and Savior, you have a choice to believe it without any material evidence, that is "faith". After believing it with your heart and admitting you need forgiveness for your sins and a Lord to lead you, you now start your journey for the rest of your life, your new birth.

You are in the beginning of your infant stage, therefore; you must become as little children in order to enter the kingdom of God. That means that all things have become new, the old things have passed away, and our old way of doing things are gone (Eph. 4:22; Col. 3:9). The old way we lived is gone (old man) and the new way of thinking, which is according to the word of God (new man), has just begun—the infant is born.

Matthew 18:2-5 says "Then Jesus called a little child to Him, set him in the midst of them, and said, "Assuredly, I say to you, unless you are converted and become as little children, you will by no means enter the kingdom of heaven. Therefore whoever humbles himself as this little child is the greatest in the kingdom of heaven."

With your quality decision to give your life to Christ and allow Him to be Lord over your life, you become a "whole person" in Christ. Without being born-again, some people act in certain ways, driven by their emotions.

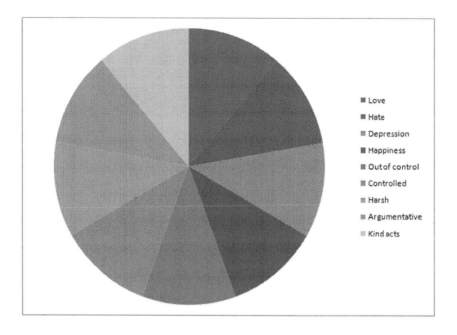

You may be a good child, but not a good student, you may be a good parent, but not a good spouse. You may be a good sibling, but not a good friend, etc. But in Christ, you have the fruit of the Holy Spirit which becomes your character (Gal. 5:22). Therefore; being a whole person in Christ, you do not get to pick and choose who you want to love or hate, neither do you get to choose which situation you will have self-control and patience in. The Word of God teaches us to do good to all men (1 Peter 3:8-12).

When you are complete in Christ, that is "a whole person", you are prepared for every good work. A double-minded man is unstable in all of his ways, making decisions without obeying the Word (James 1:8). According to the word, God has not given us a spirit of fear; but of power, and of love, and of a sound mind (2 Tim. 1:7).

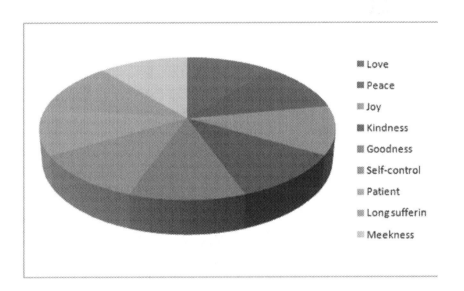

- Love
- Peace
- Joy
- Kindness
- Goodness
- Self-control
- Patient
- Long sufferin
- Meekness

_____

_____

_____

_____

_____

_____

_____

_____

_____

_____

_____

_____

_____

_____

_____

_____

_____

Chapter 2

Repentance And Confession
(The Infant Stage)

Repentance and conversion are the main two things we have to do in order to receive the Holy Spirit. Turning away from habitual sins is like cleaning the house to move the Holy Spirit in. You must feel remorse for past actions that were not of God in order to truly repent.

There was a situation with a young woman who was in a sexual relationship, without being married, and later on she married the man. Her mother told her that she needed to repent, but she did not understand what her mother meant and she answered her mother by saying "but we are married now". The problem with that is she should have felt remorse for sinning against God (having sex before marriage) and because she did not feel that remorse, she did not ask God for forgiveness for her sexual sin.

True repentance starts with remorse for past sins and causes you to convert, that is, turn in the other direction; God commands repentance. She needed to confess that

she had sinned against God and the temple of the Holy
Spirit (1 Cor. 6:18-20).

*And Acts 17:30-31 says, "In the past God overlooked such
ignorance, but now he commands all people everywhere to
repent."*

John the Baptist preached repentance, God sent him as a
forerunner for Jesus.

*Matthew 3:1-3 says, "in those days John the Baptist came,
preaching in the Desert of Judea and saying, "Repent, for
the kingdom of heaven is near."*

Jesus preached repentance, to continue what John the
Baptist started.

*Mark 1:14-15 says, "After John was put in prison, Jesus
went into Galilee, proclaiming the good news of God."
The time has come, he said. "The kingdom of God is near.
Repent and believe the good news!"*

*Revelation 3:19-20 says, "Those, whom I love I rebuke and
discipline. So be earnest, and repent."*

The disciples taught repentance to continue what Jesus taught.

> *Mark 6:8-12 says, "These were his instructions: "Take nothing for the journey except a staff--no bread, no bag, no money in your belts. Wear sandals but not an extra tunic. Whenever you enter a house, stay there until you leave that town. And if any place will not welcome you or listen to you, shake the dust off your feet when you leave, as a testimony against them." They went out and preached that people should repent."*
>
> *Acts 2:38-39 says, "Peter replied Repent and be baptized, every one of you, in the name of Jesus Christ for the forgiveness of your sins. And you will receive the gift of the Holy Spirit. The promise is for you and your children and for all who are far off—for all whom the Lord our God will call."*
>
> *Acts 3:19 says, "Repent, then, and turn to God, so that your sins may be wiped out, that times of refreshing may come from the Lord."*

You can consider repentance to be two-fold: to feel sorrow for actions or to change your mind, that is, convert-change to a different system or method.

Confession

As stated earlier, repentance is the key to receiving the infilling of the Holy Spirit. The reason it is said to be in two-fold is because, if you have no remorse for doing wrong, you will not change or be converted. Confession has to be made from your own heart to God, acknowledging your wrong before God.

Just because you get what you want, it does not mean that you felt remorse for sinning against God. We need to feel remorse for sinning against God, whether anyone knows it or not. God forbids that we continue to sin.

When no consequences for actions are received, usually it is repeated. On the other hand, when you truly feel remorse for past actions, it causes you to change your mind. In the case with the young woman, she did not feel remorse for sinning against God, she got what she ultimately wanted, which was to be his wife.

The real danger of not having any remorse is, a lack of conviction to change and usually a continuation of the behavior. It is not strange that there are almost as many divorces in Christian marriages as secular because the impenitent sexual sins just keep on. When a person is restrained from sin, because of the obedience to God, then that same reverence will continue to follow. You must do as David did and hide God's word in your heart, which will keep you from falling.

Psalms 119:11 says, "Your word I have hidden in my heart, That I might not sin against You."

Repentance does not mean that you will not be tempted, but it means that God is a greater choice that gives peace and blessings. The longer or the more you submit to God and resist the devil, he will flee from you (James 4:7). It's all about humility, which cures worldliness, because humility is a manifestation of Jesus being Lord in your life.

> *1 John 3:8-9 says, "Whoever has been born of God does not sin, for His seed remains in him; and he cannot sin, because he has been born of God."*

Change in Heart

After remorse is felt, the conversion will follow. No one desires to hurt him or herself. "Repent and be converted" is the answer. To cure the remorse is to go in another direction, not deeper into sin. God shall give you the "free gift" of the Holy Spirit to ensure that we can escape temptations. (John 14:15). When we love God, we will keep His commandments, and not continue in habitual sins, that is, you will feel remorseful when you sin (work of the Holy Spirit John 16:5-11).

True conversion is a change in heart, sin is no longer satisfying to your spirit, because you have been converted and received God's Spirit, and God is love (John 14:15-16).

John 14:21 says, "He who has My commandments and keeps them, it is he who loves Me. And he who loves Me will be loved by My Father, and I will love him and manifest Myself to him

The change in heart is because of the love for the Father. Will we sin again? Yes! But it should not be habitual sins. When we confess our sins to God and have a change in heart concerning the sin, God is faithful and just to forgive and cleanse us (1John 1:8-9). We must apply the Word to our lives daily.

Summary of the First Steps in the Right Direction.

Hear the gospel, believe it in your heart, admit that you have sinned and fallen short, repent, ask for forgiveness, and invite God in your life. Then you shall receive the 'free gift' which is the Holy Spirit.

Chapter 3

The Walk (The Toddler Stage)

To walk is to pursue a course of action or way of life, it is how we conduct ourselves. Once you have done the following it begins your new walk in Christ:

- You have heard the gospel of Jesus Christ.

- You believed it in your heart.

- You have confessed that you have sinned and fallen short of the glory.

- You have repented from your sins.

- You have invited Jesus into your heart as Lord and savior of your life.

The outward expression of your confession of Jesus being Lord of your life is water baptism. Water baptism is a symbolic act of your faith that demonstrates you are a member of the household Jesus Christ. It is the same symbolic act when Jesus was baptized by John the Baptist. You are beginning to walk and explore the things of God. In order to grow up according to God's purpose, your daily walk in Christ should include four main things:

1. Praying Without Ceasing

Praying is our way of communicating with God, talking and listening to Him. When you communicate with God, He will give you Godly wisdom for your life which causes you to make wise decisions. God communicate with us through different ways:

- Within His Spirit that indwells in you, God will speak directly to you.

- He speaks through His written word. God's Word is our daily bread, and we must read it daily just as we feed our natural body.

- He will use a chosen vessel. God will use someone to speak to you, whether it is directly or indirectly. God will confirm His Word to you, and it will agree with your spirit.

When we are putting our petitions before God, we must do it in faith. Without faith, it is impossible to please God. Speak the Word of God that speaks of His promises concerning your situation (Heb. 11:6; Rom. 1:17; 2 Cor. 5:7).

Isaiah 55:11 says, "So shall My word be that goes forth from My mouth; It shall not return to Me void, But it shall accomplish what I please, and it shall prosper in the thing for which I sent it."

Knowing God's Word allows us to know the promises that God has for us and the provision that Jesus provided for us. Knowledge is power, and we give power to our prayers when we speak the Word of God over our lives.

2. Studying the Word of God and Rightly Dividing the Word of Truth

When you study the Word of God and allow God to reveal His righteous intentions to you, you begin to increase in faith and knowledge. Studying God's Word causes you to begin to grow spiritually because faith comes by hearing the Word of God (Rom. 10:17; Heb. 11:6). Our faith in God's Word and acting on it, is like a baby's first step on his or her own. The word is a lamp to our feet because we learn to follow God by obeying His word (2 Sam. 22:29; Ps. 119:105).

In the book of John, it speaks of a baptism of the "water and the Spirit", the water in that passage of scripture is symbolic for the Word of God. Baptism means to be emerged, the Word of God must cover us. The understanding and obeying of the Word of God is your growth from infant to adult, and it will develop the "whole person" in you.

3. Worship and Praise God

God created us for His glory, which is inward and outward worship and praise. The inward worship should come before the outward worship. Worship is expressed in many different ways, for example; not having another God before Him, thanksgiving, and ceremonious prayers of adoration and sanctification.

And an outward worship is when we lift up holy hands in the sanctuary, we kneel down before Him, and we sing or speak words of adoration with our voices. Praise is very similar, but a little different here is an example of the difference in the Word of God. It says, "Let everything that have breathe praise the Lord" (Ps. 150:6). God is due all the praise regardless of who it is, or what condition it is in, but worship is more of a love thing, you do it just because you love and adore Him.

However; they interact very closely, as in expression, which could be of thanksgiving, which also could be a praise or worship. All the praise and worship belongs to God, we can praise others, but we should never worship another as God (Ex. 34:14-17).

4. Confessing Faults and repenting

We will error in this walk, whether it's by omitting to do what God said or doing what He said not to do. Jesus died to make provision for our forgiveness of sin and we can come boldly to the throne of grace (praying to the Father). We must confess or acknowledge the sins we commit so God will forgive and cleanse us (1 John 1:8-9).

When we just come clean and admit we have sinned, and then turn from the sins, a time of refreshing from God will come to us (Acts 3:19).

Brenda Duckworth

Chapter 4

The Armor of God
(The Adolescent Stage)

THE ARMOR OF GOD

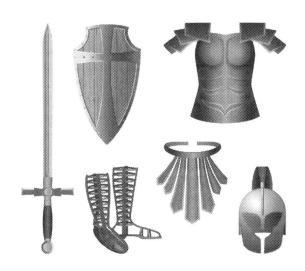

In this walk or journey of life, it does not exempt us from the wiles of the devil, but on the contrary it may intensify. In the book of Ephesians, the apostle Paul wrote to the Christians in Ephesus. Paul told them about the riches and promises they had as believers. He concluded the chapter with this, starting with verse ten, "finally".

In addition to all that Paul said prior, he allowed them to know that there was a war going on, and you must be prepared to fight and win. Going through the adolescent stage of life can be very challenging and difficult. This is a brief guideline, yet it's the most powerful, of the war and weapons we need to win. This is what we are fighting against.

Ephesians 6:10-19 says, "Finally, my brethren, be strong in the Lord and in the power of His might. Put on the whole armor of God, that you may be able to stand against the wiles of the devil. For we do not wrestle against flesh and blood, but against principalities, against powers, against the rulers of the darkness of this age, against spiritual hosts of wickedness in the heavenly places. Therefore take up the whole armor of God, that you may be able to withstand in the evil day, and having done all, to stand."

The weapon we need to win the war is the "whole armor of God", which is the Word of God, our daily bread. We have God's word, which is God, and He fights for us. That is why the Word of God says, "Heaven and earth will pass away, but my Word will forever stand." The power, promises, and way, is the Word of God.

Jesus spoke the Word only to the devil, and he left Jesus.

> *Ephesians 6:14-18 says "Stand therefore, having girded your waist with truth, having put on the breastplate of righteousness, and having shod your feet with the preparation of the gospel of peace; above all, taking the shield of faith with which you will be able to quench all the fiery darts of the wicked one. And take the helmet of salvation, and the sword of the Spirit, which is the word of God; praying always with all prayer and supplication in the Spirit, being watchful to this end with all perseverance and supplication for all the saints"*

This is like our adolescent stage of life sayings; "no one understands me", "I don't have any friends", "things are always going wrong", "everyone picks on me". I am here to tell you, when you leave Satan, he does everything he can and uses anyone he can to get you back. The saying, "when I got saved, all hell broke loose," is true. When you were not saved, you were in a Spiritual war, you just did not know it, and you were not fighting it. A Spiritual war has been going on since the beginning of time, when God kicked Satan out of heaven the war began.

As a matter of fact, it becomes more intensified because you are learning what this world is all about, which is: your purpose, identifying the enemy and how to fight and win. The main thing you need to know in this chapter is that, we are not fighting against flesh-and-blood (people), but we are battling against rulers of darkness, powers, and principalities.

The word *principality* means an area that a prince controls. A prince is a monarch or king, that is, someone who rules. Well, Satan is the prince of evil, he rules the kingdom of darkness (sin). The good news is that, because of Jesus, we have overcome the evil one. Jesus prayed that God would keep us from the evil one (John 17:15-16). Because Jesus has prayed to the Father for us, the apostle Paul reminded us of God's faithfulness to guard us from the evil one by putting on the whole armor of God.

> *2 Thessalonians 3:3 says, "But the Lord is faithful, who will establish you and guard you from the evil one." Looking at the armor of God piece by piece, you will see all of it is the Word of God.*

1. Gird Your Waist With The Belt Of Truth

The word *gird* means surround, encircle, or bind. We use a belt as a gird. We put on a belt to ensure support or safety. Another translation says, "gird up your loins with the belt of truth." Loins are the places in your body that can be easily penetrated. Therefore, we need to take extra precautions to protect them. Your spiritual loins may be something different from others, and could be anything that easily penetrates you in a negative way, such as, looks, stature, intellect, and so forth.

However, you need reinforcement with the truth, which is God's word (John. 8:32, 17:17; Eph. 1:13). I will give you an example of something that concerned me that needed to be girded up with the belt of truth, my integrity as a woman of God.

Satan is forever trying to discredit me concerning who I am in Christ. My character and integrity is attacked all the time. Satan knows that character and integrity are very important to me because of the sake of the gospel. Therefore, I have to constantly speak the Word of God to myself, and continue to be who I am according to God, not what people are saying or will assert.

We need to go to God and ask, "who do you say I am?" and the Holy Spirit will reveal to you who you are. God is able to search the heart and the intent. Gird up your loins with the belt of truth. When God shows you your error, repent, or if someone has wronged you, forgive. Forgiveness is given to you from the Father. There is now no condemnation to those who are in Christ (those who have been born again and Christ is Lord of their lives. Rom. 8:1).

2. Breastplate of Righteousness

When we think of a "breastplate," we usually envision something that covers the chest, such as a bullet-proof vest. Spiritually, when we think of the heart, the issues of life flows from it (Prov. 4:23; Matt. 15-18-19). Usually the way we have been raised or how circumstances have shaped us, are the way we live; according to our thinking, it is right and we believe it is our heart. That type of righteousness is called "self-righteous".

Therefore, you must put on the "righteousness of God", doing the right thing according to God's Word that pertains to situations in our lives. Once again, it is the ways of the Lord, not our way, His ways are not like our ways, and His thoughts are not our thoughts (Isa. 55:8).

3. Shod Your Feet With the Preparation

of the Gospel of Peace

The word *shod* in the Greek language means bind. Shod means it had a better grip or secure grip, to make sure your sandals are bound. Shod your feet means to be rooted and grounded in the Word of God concerning the news about Jesus Christ. So many things are being said and done in the name of "church, Christianity, and denomination (doctrinal names)," but through all of your getting, you should get the truth of God's Word concerning Jesus. You cannot get to God except through His son, Jesus Christ.

John 14:6 says, "Jesus said to him, "I am the way, the truth, and the life. No one comes to the Father except through Me."

To shod your feet with the preparation of the gospel of peace is to know the Word concerning Jesus Christ, by studying to show yourself approved (2 Tim. 2:15). Jesus is the way, the truth, and the life.

4. Shield of Faith

Shield usually causes us to think of some type of protection or covering from harm or danger. The definition of shield is, *a device or part that serves as a protective cover or barrier.* The Word is the covering or protection of our faith in the gospel of Jesus Christ. When we do not feel that God is with us, or hear us, or when what we see does not look good, we must remember what faith is, it is not what you can see with the natural eyes; nor is it what we feel in our emotions. Faith is the facts concerning Jesus and His promises to us.

In the book of Hebrews the author gives a biblical definition of faith (Heb. 11:1). Faith is when we cannot see it, but it manifests into substance, things we can see. Not one of us was there when Jesus died on the cross, but we all had to believe the Word concerning Him without any material evidence. We all started with the same measure of faith, "believe that Jesus is the Son of God, He was crucified, buried and God raised Him from the dead". If the devil gets us to deny that truth, we will lose our shield of faith that protects us. If we lose our faith, we are uncovered and open for all attacks or wiles of the devil (John- 3:17-18).

Ephesians 2:8-10 says, "For by grace you have been saved through faith, and that not of yourselves; it is the gift of God, not of works, lest anyone should boast."

It is the faith that we are saved through. The word through is a function word used to indicate a passage from one end or a boundary to another. No matter what the devil is doing, we must shield ourselves with the Word of God. Our faith gets us through the wiles of the devil.

5. Helmet of Salvation

When we use the word *helmet,* it means some protection of the head. We have to know the truth, which will set us free. Faith in God's Word causes us to believe unto salvation, saved from sin and destruction. No matter what comes or what maybe said, we must put on the helmet of salvation, which is, knowing the Word and rightly dividing the truth. Knowing the Word, believing it in your heart, repenting of sins, forgiving others, rightly dividing, and obeying the Word of Truth, gives us our helmet of salvation.

6. Sword of the Spirit

The word *sword* is usually associated with a fight, not only a skirmish, but a battle to do some damage. The definition for sword is a weapon with a long blade for cutting or thrusting, often used as a symbol of honor and authority. God's Word is the authority on this earth and in heaven, therefore, the word is God (John 1:1) and it cuts as a two-edge sword.

Hebrews 4:12-13 says, "For the word of God is living and powerful, and sharper than any two-edged sword, piercing even to the division of soul and spirit, and of joints and marrow, and is a discerner of the thoughts and intents of the heart. And there is no creature hidden from His sight, but all things are naked and open to the eyes of Him to whom we must give account."

The Word of God is our daily bread that governs everything in our lives and we cannot live without it (John 6:48).

John 6:35 says, "And Jesus said to them, "I am the bread of life. He who comes to Me shall never hunger, and he who believes in Me shall never thirst."

The Word, heals, delivers, convicts, gives new and abundant life, revives, refreshes, increases faith, and provides power. Our weapons are not carnal, but they are mighty in tearing down strongholds. You will always have victory in your fight, if you put on the whole armor of God. Remember, victory is after a struggle, if there is no struggle, there will be no victory. The Word of God pertains to every situation that you will face.

Chapter 5

The Gifts and Callings or Talents (The Adult Stage)

As you have gone through the first three stages in your

new birth (infant, toddler, and adolescent), you become a

mature Christian. Now you know your purpose and the plans that God has for you, mostly through your gifts and callings. There are many gifts and callings, most people are multi-talented or gifted.

In Genesis 1:26-28, God said to mankind, to be fruitful and multiply and to replenish the earth, and God has given us all we need to carry out His purpose by giving gifts and talents. Remember, God is above all, and works through all (Eph. 4:4-6). Scripture speaks of gifts, and callings of God are irrevocable, God gave them when you were in your mother's womb (Rom. 11:29).

These are eight gifts that God has appointed in the church.

1 Corinthians 12:27-31 says, "Now you are the body of Christ, and members individually. And God has appointed these in the church: first apostles, second prophets, third teachers, after that miracles, then gifts of healings, helps, administrations, varieties of tongues. Are all apostles? Are all prophets? Are all teachers? Are all workers of miracles? Do all have gifts of healings? Do all speak with tongues? Do all interpret? But earnestly desire the best gifts. And yet I show you a more excellent way.

The gifts or talents of helps and administrations are unlimited, and no one was left out. However, God made Christ the head of the church, neither male nor female is head of the church, but Christ is by God's choosing. The five gifts that Jesus gave for the church that are mentioned in Ephesians 4:7-11.

Ephesians 4:7-16 says, "But to each one of us grace was given according to the measure of Christ's gift. Therefore He says:, "He led captivity captive, "When He ascended on high, and gave gifts to men."(Now this, "He ascended" --what does it mean, but that He also first descended into the lower parts of the earth? He who descended is also the One who ascended far above all the heavens, that He might fill all things.) And He Himself gave some to be apostles, some prophets, some evangelists, and some pastors and teachers, that we should no longer be children, tossed to and fro and carried about with every wind of doctrine, by the trickery of men, in the cunning craftiness of deceitful plotting, but, speaking the truth in love, may grow up in all things into Him who is the head—Christ--.

The five gifts that Jesus gave was His choice of who received those gifts, not man's choice. Often times we have heard or were taught that certain gifts were not given to females, Jesus made that decision all by Himself. We know why Jesus gave us special abilities or talents, to carry out purpose.

> *Ephesians 4:12-13 says, "For the equipping of the saints for the work of ministry, for the edifying of the body of Christ, 'till we all come to the unity of the faith and of the knowledge of the Son of God, to a perfect man, to the measure of the stature of the fullness of Christ."*

- **Apostle**—*means one who is sent.*

The function of an apostle is one who goes where Christ is not known and preaches the doctrine of Jesus Christ. He or she causes the unbeliever to become a believer. In scripture, it is written as "first Apostles" the gift of an apostle has to go forth before we have a need for a pastor.

- **Pastor**— *means one who acts as a shepherd.*

A shepherd cares for sheep that belongs to someone else. The people belongs to God and the pastor is a Spiritual overseer. The function is to feed with wisdom and knowledge and then, guide and provide ultimate care.

- **Prophet**— *means one chosen to speak the will and Word of God.*

We have God's written word, but we also need a Word from the prophets of God (a human speaking).

- **Evangelist/Preacher**— *means one who proclaims the gospel of Jesus Christ.*

They are gifted with their experiences with God to cause others to accept Christ as their personal Lord and Savior.

- **Teacher**—*one who is gifted to teach. One who relays information to others especially written concepts.*

Jesus gave these five gifts for the Church, however, there are other gifts and callings. When each of us uses our gifts and talents according to the will of God, the church will prosper.

The Holy Spirit gives nine gifts. These are the gifts that you may not have ever operated in until you received the Holy Spirit, after new birth.

> *1 Corinthians 12:4-11 says "there are diversities of gifts, but the same Spirit. There are differences of ministries, but the same Lord. And there are diversities of activities, but it is the same God who works all in all. But the manifestation of the Spirit is given to each one for the profit of all: 8 for to one is given the word of wisdom through the Spirit, to another the word of knowledge through the same Spirit, to another faith by the same Spirit, to another gifts of healings by the same Spirit,-to another the working of miracles, to another prophecy, to another discerning of spirits, to another different kinds of tongues, to another the interpretation of tongues. But one and the same Spirit works all these things, distributing to each one individually as He wills."*

Summary of Gifts and Callings:

There are eight gifts from the father, these are gifts without repentance, and they are irrevocable (you are born with them, it is your calling). When we spoke earlier concerning God who foreknew us, He gave the following gifts before we were placed in our mother's womb:

- Apostles

- Prophets

- Teachers

- Workers of miracles

- Hospitality

- Administration

- Gifts of healings

- Varieties of tongues

The five gifts that Jesus gave for the church (five-fold ministry gifts) are:

- Apostles

- Prophets

- Pastors

- Evangelists or Preachers

- Teachers

The Holy spirit gives the following nine gifts after a new birth, and they are available to all believers as the holy spirit wills:

- Wisdom

- Knowledge

- Faith

- Prophecy

- Workers of miracles

- Gifts of healings

- Discerning of spirits

- Diversities of tongues

- Interpretation of tongues

The greatest gifts that were given to us are, grace and the Holy Spirit.

_____

_____

_____

_____

_____

_____

_____

_____

_____

_____

_____

_____

_____

_____

_____

_____

_____

Chapter 6

Power, Promises, and Benefits (PPB)

In the book of Genesis (1:26-28) God gave man dominion over the things He created, the plan of God for man. When God raised Jesus from the dead, He rose with all authority in heaven and on earth (Matthew 28:18) and through Jesus we have that same authority. God made us co-heirs with Christ Jesus (Rom. 8:17) and the right to cry "abba" which means father (Rom. 8:15; Galatians. 4:6).

In the book of Ephesians, Paul was talking to the Christians at Ephesus and he wanted them to know their inheritances in Christ. Paul wanted them to know that the blessings were unlimited, he said "now unto him who is able to do exceedingly, abundantly more than we can ask or think". At the end of that scripture it stated "according to the power that works within you", therefore, we need to know the power, promises and benefits of God.

Often time we are just so happy to be saved, but not being aware of the power, promises and benefits we have in Christ Jesus. I am going to mention a few, but it is enough to make you aware of many promises and benefits we have. I am going to talk about the power we have first, because God knew that we would need His power to walk this walk and receive the crown of life.

When Jesus walked with the disciples for forty days after He was resurrected from the dead, He told them that they would receive power after the Holy Ghost came upon them.

Acts 1:8 says, "but you shall receive power when the Holy Spirit has come upon you; and you shall be witnesses to Me in Jerusalem, and in all Judea and Samaria, and to the end of the earth."

- **Power to Trample Over The Enemy**

Luke 10:19 says "Behold, I give you the authority to trample on serpents and scorpions, and over all the power of the enemy, and nothing shall by any means hurt you."

The enemy is any and all of Satan's wiles, remember we have one enemy and that is Satan, He uses sin to entice us. But through Jesus Christ, we have a way to escape, no matter what temptation may come, we have the power to overcome it (1 John 2:13-14).

> *1 Corinthians 10:13 says, "No temptation has overtaken you except such as is common to man; but God is faithful, who will not allow you to be tempted beyond what you are able, but with the temptation will also make the way of escape, that you may be able to bear it.*

- **Power to Overcome the World**

Satan is in control of the world's systems and God has given us the power over His system. There are certain things set up in the world that are against the knowledge of God, for instance, no prayer in school, taking Christ out of Christmas and the list goes on, but we have the victory in our lives through Jesus Christ.

> *1 John 4:4 says, "You are of God, little children, and have overcome them, because He who is in you is greater than he who is in the world.*
>
> *John 16:33 "These things I have spoken to you, that in Me you may have peace. In the world you will have tribulation; but be of good cheer, I have overcome the world."*

Everything Jesus did, He died for us so that we could do the same and greater works than He did, but we must be born again.

> *John 14:12-14 "Most assuredly, I say to you, he who believes in Me, the works that I do he will do also; and greater works than these he will do, because I go to My Father. 13 And whatever you ask in My name, that I will do, that the Father may be glorified in the Son. 14 If you ask anything in My name, I will do it.*

- **Power Over Unclean Spirit**

Jesus gave the twelve disciples the power over unclean spirits when He sent them out, now because you have been born again, you have that same power.

> *Matthew 10:1 says, "And when He had called His twelve disciples to Him, He gave them power over unclean spirits, to cast them out, and to heal all kinds of sickness and all kinds of disease.*

- **Power to Witness**

> *Acts 1:8 "But you shall receive power when the Holy Spirit has come upon you; and you shall be witnesses to Me in Jerusalem, and in all Judea and Samaria, and to the end of the earth."*

- **Power to Fight, Using Your Spiritual Weapons**

You have the ability to stop the thoughts that the enemy gives to you, sin starts with a thought. If we do not cast down vain thoughts and imaginations, they can bring forth sin.

> 2 Corinthians 10:4-6 *"For the weapons of our warfare are not carnal but mighty in God for pulling down strongholds, casting down arguments and every high thing that exalts itself against the knowledge of God, bringing every thought into captivity to the obedience of Christ, and being ready to punish all disobedience when your obedience is fulfilled.*

The Promises of God

The promises of God are yes and amen, meaning every promise that God gave, He shall bring to pass. In the book of Psalms (34:20), it speaks of Jesus guarding His bones and not one is broken, in this passage the word "bones" is symbolizing "promises" of God through Jesus—not one promise was broken. And if you are Christ's, then you are Abraham's seed, and heirs according to the promise (Galatians. 3:29).

- **Eternal Life**

> *John 3:14-16 "And as Moses lifted up the serpent in the wilderness, even so must the Son of Man be lifted up, that whoever believes in Him should not perish but have eternal life."*

> *1 John 2:24 "And this is the promise that He has promised us—eternal life."*

> *Titus 1:1-2 "God's elect and the acknowledgment of the truth which accords with godliness, in hope of eternal life which God, who cannot lie, promised before time began."*

- **Forgiveness of Sins**

God has promised to forgive us of all our sins, if we confess them. As stated earlier, we must admit that we have sinned and God is faithful and just to forgive us and cleanse us.

> *Matthew 6:14 "For if you forgive men their trespasses, your heavenly Father will also forgive you."*
>
> *Ephesians 1:7-8 "In Him we have redemption through His blood, the forgiveness of sins, according to the riches of His grace which He made to abound toward us in all wisdom and prudence,"*

- **Deliverance from Afflictions**

In this walk we are afflicted in many areas of our lives, emotionally, physically, socially, economically and spiritually—but God has a way of deliverance for us as long as we acknowledge Him in all our ways (Ps. 34:19).

> *Colossians 1:13-14 "He has delivered us from the power of darkness and conveyed us into the kingdom of the Son of His love, in whom we have redemption through His blood, the forgiveness of sins."*

- **Removal of Obstacles**

We know that obstacles are things that makes it difficult to do something, but we have the promise of God to remove them all. In the gospel of Matthews it speaks of having the faith in God, even if it is a small amount, things will be moved (Matthew 17:20). It doesn't always come right away, but with fasting and praying.

Matthew 21:21-22 "So Jesus answered and said to them, "Assuredly, I say to you, if you have faith and do not doubt, you will not only do what was done to the fig tree, but also if you say to this mountain, 'Be removed and be cast into the sea,' it will be done. And whatever things you ask in prayer, believing, you will receive."

Luke 17:6 "So the Lord said, "If you have faith as a mustard seed, you can say to this mulberry tree, 'Be pulled up by the roots and be planted in the sea,' and it would obey you."

The key to receive this this type of promise is faith in God's Word. Knowing the will of God for your life and believing it and not doubting, it shall be done. Faith works patience in us, Abraham believed God when He said He was going to give him a son, although it took 25 years to manifest (Genesis 12:21).

- **Infinite Value**

We know that infinite means having no limits, well God has no limits. He protects and provides in ways we do not comprehend nor will we ever really know. In the book of Isaiah, He tells us, His ways are not our ways.

> *Isaiah 55:8-11 "For my thoughts are not your thoughts, neither are your ways my ways," declares the Lord.*
>
> *"As the heavens are higher than the earth, so are my ways higher than your ways and my thoughts than your thoughts. As the rain and the snow come down from heaven, and do not return to it without watering the earth and making it bud and flourish, so that it yields seed for the sower and bread for the eater, so is my word that goes out from my mouth: It will not return to me empty, but will accomplish what I desire and achieve the purpose for which I sent it.*

God is able to fulfill all of His promises, every word that proceeds from His mouth.

Benefits of God

We did not deserve all that God has granted us unconditionally. When we do things to people, especially over a period of time, we lose certain benefits with them but we do not lose these benefits of God. These are some of the benefits that God has granted to us. When we define benefit, it is an act of kindness.

- **Love of God**

God's love is unconditionally, God gave His only son for the love He has for us. And while we were yet sinning, Jesus died for us. There is no greater love than the love of the Father and His Son. God gave his son and his son gave his life for us.

John 3:16 "For God so loved the world that He gave His only begotten Son, that whoever believes in Him should not perish but have everlasting life."

Galatians 2:20 "I have been crucified with Christ; it is no longer I who live, but Christ lives in me; and the life which I now live in the flesh I live by faith in the Son of God, who loved me and gave Himself for me."

- **Grace of God**

God's grace is a gift, there is nothing we could have done to deserve all that God has done and is still doing for us. All that we have in God, through Christ, is all by grace and not by works. The means of our salvation is by Grace.

Ephesians 2:8-10 "For by grace you have been saved through faith, and that not of yourselves; it is the gift of God, not of works, lest anyone should boast."

- **Peace of God**

God gives us peace in situations that no one can give to us. When we are going through hard times it is very important to have the peace of God. Peace is a power of sustaining patient, when we are over anxious it can cause more damage to the situation. My sister was going through a very difficult time when she went in to have surgery that should have been a three day stay, but it turned out to be three weeks. There were so many things that went wrong and she began to have anxiety attacks, but God spoke to her and said He was taking care of her and then she received the peace of God that helped her get through a very difficult time.

> *Philippians 4:6-7 "Be anxious for nothing, but in everything by prayer and supplication, with thanksgiving, let your requests be made known to God; and the peace of God, which surpasses all understanding, will guard your hearts and minds through Christ Jesus."*

All that we are in Christ Jesus, which is, co-heirs with Him. They are all benefits that God has given to us.

Galatians 3:26-28 "For you are all sons of God through faith in Christ Jesus. For as many of you as were baptized into Christ have put on Christ. There is neither Jew nor Greek, there is neither slave nor free, there is neither male nor female; for you are all one in Christ Jesus.

Galatians 4:4-7 "But when the fullness of the time had come, God sent forth His Son, born of a woman, born under the law, to redeem those who were under the law, that we might receive the adoption as sons.

And because you are sons, God has sent forth the Spirit of His Son into your hearts, crying out, "Abba, Father!" Therefore you are no longer a slave but a son, and if a son, then an heir of God through Christ."

In conclusion of this book, we have everything we need in Christ Jesus—to know this and experience it is being born-again. When one is not born-again, Satan speaks lies, creates situations and he tells you that you are defeated. After reading this book you shall know the truth and the truth shall set you free. You must acknowledge God in all your ways and He shall direct your path, allow Him to lead. My life would have not been what it is without my new birth. Remember, God sent Jesus so that we would be whole in Him, a " whole person", to be fruitful and multiply.

Prayerfully, after reading this book, you will know your gifts, talents and callings. As you discover your gifts, understand your calling, and walk out your assignment, you will live a purpose driven life.

My Prayer for The Readers

God bless the readers with blessings and give them the strength to subdue the earth, to overcome every plan of the evil one, to walk in purpose, to be a witness for you and to keep sharing this information with others so that they will be fruitful and multiply.

Brenda Duckworth

Glossary

Merriam-Webster Dictionary

Admit—*to concede as truth or valid*

Baptism—*purification by or submergence in Spirit.*

Birth—*the beginning or origin of something*

Call—*to make a request or demand*

Child—*an unborn or recently born person; a young person especially between infancy and youth*

Confess—*to tell or make known*

Converted—*to change from one form or use to another*

Dedication—*a devoting or setting aside for a particular purpose*

Fellowship—*companionship, company; community of interest, activity, feeling, or experience; the state of being a fellow.*

Fellow—*a member of a group having common characteristics*

Guilt—*the state of one who has committed an offense especially consciously*

Invite-- *to request the presence or participation of; to urge politely.*

Life—*the ability to grow, change, etc.; the experience of being alive*

Loin—*the upper and lower abdominal regions and the region about the hips*

Lord—*one having power and authority over others*

New—*having recently come into existence*

Principality—*the territory or jurisdiction of a prince: the country that gives title to a prince.*

Relationship—*the way in which two or more people or things are connected; a state of affairs existing between those having relations or dealings.*

Remorse—*a feeling of being sorry for doing something bad or wrong in the past; a feeling of guilt.*

Repent—*to feel or show that you are sorry for something bad or wrong that you did and that you want to do what is right; to turn from sin and dedicate oneself to the amendments of one's life; to feel regret or contrition.*

Savior—*one that saves from danger or destruction*

Shield—*a device or part that serves as a protective cover or barrier*

Walk—*to pursue a course of action or way of life; conduct oneself*

Whole—*complete or full; not lacking or leaving out any part; having all the parts; not divided or cut into pieces.*

Worship—*reverence offered a divine being or supernatural power; also: an act expressing such reverence*

Printed in the United States
By Bookmasters